UNDERCURRENTS Series Editor J.J. Lee

Divorce in Ireland: Who Should Bear the Cost?

PETER WARD

CORK UNIVERSITY PRESS

First published in 1993 by
Cork University Press
University College
Cork
Ireland

British Library Cataloguing in Publication Data

A CIP catalogue record for this book is available from the British Library

ISBN 0 902561 69 3

Typeset in Ireland by Seton Music Graphics Ltd, Co. Cork
Printed in Ireland by ColourBooks, Baldoyle, Co. Dublin

CONTENTS

ACKNOWLEDGEMENTS

I wish to thank Joe Lee for emboldening me to write this pamphlet for the *Undercurrents* series. I owe a debt of gratitude to Sara Wilbourne of Cork University Press for her expert advice, support and good humour throughout the task. I wish, finally, to express my thanks to my colleagues, academic and secretarial, in the Department of Law, UCC for their assistance, encouragement and friendship.

Peter Ward
June 1993

1. INTRODUCTION

'Divorce impoverishes women and children – Vote No'. Thus ran one of the most dominant slogans of the anti-divorce lobby during the 1986 referendum campaign. The Tenth Amendment of the Constitution Bill 1986 proposed that the prohibition on divorce, contained in Article 41.3.2,[1] be deleted from the constitution and replaced by a provision allowing for the dissolution of marriage in specified circumstances.[2] On the 26 June 1986 the proposal was rejected by 63.5 per cent of those who voted in the referendum.[3] While it is impossible to state the precise reasons of those who rejected the introduction of divorce, what is certain is that the issue of the financial consequences of divorce played a central role in the debate prior to the referendum.[4] The spectre of poverty-stricken wives and children discarded by callous husbands and fathers was invoked as an inevitable concomitant of the right to have one's marriage dissolved. The retention of the constitutional ban on divorce, it was argued, was the only means of preventing the propulsion of innocent victims into penury.

The proponents of divorce argued that it was the separation of the spouses and not the dissolution of the marriage which caused financial hardship. Further, they argued, the enshrinement in the Constitution of the requirement that a court granting a decree be 'satisfied that adequate and proper provision having regard to the circumstances will be made for any dependent spouse and for any child who is dependent on either spouse', protected dependants as far as possible from such consequences. In so far as this issue was decisive of the outcome of the referendum, however, the pro-divorce lobby failed to allay the fears raised by those opposed to the reform.

This aspect of the divorce debate was more remarkable for what was omitted than for what was encompassed within it. It was conducted in the absence of any detailed empirical data on the financial circumstances of separated spouses in Ireland – indeed even the

1

number of separated spouses in Ireland was subject to widely differing estimates.[5] No evidence was available as to how family law operates in practice in this country, yet assumptions were made that existing statutory remedies operated well. Further, there was neither detailed discussion nor any seeming appreciation of how social welfare law interacts with family law in the area of financial provision for separated spouses. The renewed debate on divorce in Ireland need not be so ill informed. More detailed information is available on the extent of marriage breakdown in this country; empirical evidence of how our statutory remedies work in practice has come to light for the first time; and international trends in child support policy have focussed more sharply on the relationship between social security payments and maintenance.

The long-awaited White Paper on divorce, finally published in September 1992 under the title *Marital Breakdown — A Review and Proposed Changes* envisaged another referendum on divorce before the end of 1993 and it set out five alternative constitutional provisions which would allow for the introduction of divorce. It also, as its title suggests, encompasses a review of Irish family law and makes wide-ranging proposals for legislative reform both pursuant to and independently of possible constitutional change. The Minister for Equality and Law Reform has most recently announced that a referendum will be held in the first half of 1994. In an effort to avoid the 'muddying of the waters' in relation to property and maintenance matters which he claimed to have occured in 1986, he has promised to publish a bill before the referendum setting out the grounds on which divorce will be available and the consequences which will flow from divorce in matters such as property, maintenance and social welfare.

The immediate response of the anti-divorce lobby to the publication of the White Paper has been to return once more to those arguments which proved so effective on their last outing and thus to reiterate the conviction that divorce would cause poverty for women and children and, on this ground alone, should be resisted. It is argued that the White Paper contains nothing to assuage fears of the disastrous economic consequences which divorce guarantees. The proponents of divorce immediately rebutted once more with the contention that it is the separation of the spouses and not their divorce which precipitates any financial crisis and, most importantly, the law relating to the property and financial rights of spouses has been fundamentally altered in the period since 1986, in particular as a result of the Judicial Separation and Family Law Reform Act 1989, and that the fears of insufficient legal protection for the wife and children can now be shown to be unfounded.

It is to be hoped that the revived debate will prove to be a better-informed exercise than its infamous predecessor and the purpose of this publication is to make some contribution towards that goal. Ominous signs have already come to light, however, that the half-truths and deceptions that characterized this issue in 1986 are being dusted off in preparation for leading roles in the sequel.

It is simply wrong to state that divorce, of itself, causes poverty for women and children. If the standard of living of either or both parties falls after the breakdown of a marriage – as we shall see it so often does – it is the separation of the spouses and the establishment of two separate households where previously there was one which has the most obvious economic impact. Marriage breakdown is an established and thriving phenomenon in Irish family life and thus the financial crisis heralded by separation is likewise an established feature of our society. The belief that the retention of the constitutional ban on divorce in some way renders us immune from the deleterious financial consequences of marriage breakdown raises our capacity for self-deception to new and dizzying heights.

The financial consequences of the breakdown of a marriage are directly affected by the introduction of divorce in one important respect. The dissolution of a marriage and the right to remarry allows a person to undertake the obligation to maintain a second spouse, with an obvious potential impact on the resources available to meet the obligations owed to the first spouse and children. The absence of divorce does not, however, prevent a person whose marriage has broken down from incurring further financial obligations towards any children of second or further relationships. It is important to attempt to determine the unavoidable impact of the divorce itself on the financial arrangements to be made after separation. The question of distribution is most often a question of establishing priorities. The obligation to support the children of the first marriage can, for example as it is now in the United Kingdom, be given precedence over the obligation to support one's second spouse. In any event, if stark predictions are being made about the financial impact of divorce, it might be expected that the nature and extent of the obligation to support one's spouse would be a matter of some clarity. In Ireland, however, this is by no means the case and the maintenance and property rights of spouses as between themselves is the subject of renewed debate.

One is tempted to state simply that the question of the retention of the constitutional prohibition on divorce should now be debated entirely independently of the issue of the regulation of the economic consequences of marriage breakdown. While any divorce laws would of course play a central role in such regulation, their nature and effect is surely something to be determined only *after* the question of whether our society will provide for the dissolution of a marriage under any circumstances has been resolved. This dissociation of issues becomes more obvious when one considers whether those who have opposed divorce on this ground would support its introduction if assured beyond doubt that no-one would suffer financially as a result of a dissolution. In most instances the organized opposition to reform is rooted in concerns other than those financial and it is upon these that the debate would more profitably focus.

It is inevitable, however, that such dissociation will prove impossible to achieve. It is already the case that the White Paper on divorce sets out legislative proposals governing financial and property matters after the introduction of divorce and the Minister has promised that the reforms in this area will be publicized in advance of the referendum. The White Paper sets out five possible approaches to a constitutional amendment providing for the introduction of divorce. Four of the five proposed amendments incorporate the actual grounds upon which a divorce could be granted: the absence of a normal marital relationship for five years; separation for five years; judicial separation or entitlement thereto plus a period of two years; and irretrievable breakdown on proof of specified 'fault' and 'no fault' grounds. The fifth proposed amendment allows simply for the provision of divorce subject to any conditions prescribed by law. It is this latter course which represents the most legally appropriate method of allowing for the introduction of divorce in Ireland. As the White Paper itself acknowledges in assessing the relative merits of the approaches, the Constitution is more properly concerned with statements of fundamental principle rather than the detail of the law. The incorporation of such detail into the Constitution as four of the approaches require would restrain the legislature in its attempts to adapt to social change which could only be loosened by further referendums.

The demand for divorce is obvious in Irish society and this writer is of the view that its introduction is long overdue and that it is a matter for the legislature to determine the grounds upon which a divorce should be granted and, further, to regulate the economic consequences of a such a decree. These issues are destined to be intertwined and it is because of this reality that one reluctantly sets about an examination of the regulation of the financial consequences of marriage breakdown in the context of a debate on the removal of the constitutional ban on divorce.

This paper starts from the position that the anti-divorce lobby is wrong to claim that divorce will impoverish women and children in this country. Women and children are in poverty *already* in this country after marriage breakdown. Indeed, it is ironic that the absence of divorce actually deprives separated women of one possible route out of poverty – remarriage. The research from other countries which is invoked by anti-divorce campaigners in support of their argument reveals low amounts of maintenance awarded in favour of divorced spouses and children, high rates of default on such orders, and high rates of dependence on social security payments. Yet the research on the operation of Irish maintenance law in the absence of divorce reveals identical characteristics to those found abroad after divorce. The problems which we are exhorted to avoid · by retaining the constitutional ban exist already. It is towards the resolution of those problems that we must thus now look.

The Judicial Separation and Family Law Reform Act 1989 constitutes an important reform of Irish family law and it grants wide powers to the courts to make financial and property orders after a decree of judicial separation has been granted. It does not, however, provide the comprehensive answer to financial problems after separation which some pro-divorce campaigners have been tempted to claim for it. The debate in this area has avoided the fundamental questions to which the phenomenon of poverty of women and children after marriage breakdown gives rise. At the broadest level, the debate demands an examination of sex-roles and the relative economic impotence of women in Irish society, which examination is outside the scope of this paper. In more specific terms, but ones which can only be understood in the broader context, one must determine the nature of the obligation to maintain one's spouse and one's children; the effect which the dissolution of a marriage ought to have on such an obligation; the most equitable and effective means of enforcing the obligation; and the role of the state in providing for parties to marriage breakdown. It is towards these issues that attention must be focused if a comprehensive legislative response to the problem is genuinely sought.

2. THE EXTENT OF MARRIAGE BREAKDOWN IN IRELAND

While the focus of this discussion is on financial provision for spouses or ex-spouses and their children, the law and policy in relation to lone parents generally is of central importance to our main enquiry. The recognition of lone parents as a distinct group with common problems and needs, irrespective of the cause of the lone parenthood, has led to policy initiatives and reforms aimed at the group as a whole.

The national census of 1986 included for the first time the category of 'separated' person in its question on marital status and revealed 37,245 persons who described themselves as such, 14,638 males and 22,607 females.[6] The 1991 Labour Force Survey showed a figure of 46,700 separated persons in the state.[7] The White Paper on divorce concedes, however, that these figures may understate the true position. The 1991 Census figures, published after the White Paper, reveal 55,143 persons who describe themselves as separated, 21,350 males and 33,793 females.[8] This represents an increase of almost 50 per cent over the 1986 figures. The numbers of women in receipt of deserted wive's payments has increased dramatically over the past decade. Between 1981 and 1991 the number of women in receipt of deserted wife's benefit more than trebled from 3,124 to 11,358.[9] The number of women in receipt of the unmarried mother's allowance (now lone parent's allowance) over the same period increased from 4,041 to 16,564 – an increase of over 400 per cent. This can be explained by the increase in the number of births outside marriage and the decrease in the number of such children placed for adoption. In 1981 there were 3,914 births outside marriage, representing 5.4 per cent of all births. In 1991 the number of births outside marriage was 8,766 – equivalent to 16.6 per cent of all births.[10]

Marriage breakdown is clearly a significant and growing phenomenon in Ireland. In this respect family structures in Ireland are simply following, albeit at a slower rate, established trends in other Western societies. The number of lone-parent families in most Western countries has risen sharply over the past two decades and a major reason for this rise is marital dissolution. It is estimated that 10 per cent of all families in Ireland are headed by a lone parent.[11] This places us just below the European Community average of 11 per cent which ranges from the UK and Denmark with 15–17 per cent at one end to Greece, Spain and Italy with 5–6 per cent at the other end. It is thus clear that in spite of the special status bestowed upon the married family in the Constitution, which incorporates a ban on divorce, we are experiencing the same demographic trends which have precipitated fundamental reviews of family policy in other western countries.

The introduction of no-fault divorce in most western countries since the late nineteen sixties gave rise to prolonged and sustained debate on the principles which should govern post-divorce maintenance obligations. Attention was focused, in particular, on the nature of the obligation of a person to support a former spouse after the dissolution of the marriage. The rise in the number of lone-parent families and the consequent rise in public expenditure due to the high rate of dependence of lone parents upon social security payments has, more recently, given rise to debate on, and reform of, the law governing the obligation to support one's children. The evidence uncovered in other countries of how their divorce laws operate in practice has resulted in fundamental reassessment of the principles governing support obligations. This empirical evidence, upon parts of which such tendentious reliance is placed by those who oppose divorce here, can only be understood in the context of an assessment of how our laws operate in the absence of divorce.

Empirical evidence of the financial circumstances of divorced spouses and their children in England has led researchers to the conclusion that the issue of whether or not a former wife should have the right to life-long maintenance 'has little or no relevance for the great majority of the divorcing population'.[12] There is a need to examine the legal regulation of the financial relationship of separating spouses in Ireland and to compare, in like manner, the legal rhetoric with the practical experience.

EMPIRICAL EVIDENCE IN THE UNITED KINGDOM AND THE UNITED STATES

For over twenty years, research in England on the practical operation of family law has consistently highlighted the low amounts of maintenance awarded by the courts, the high rate of default on maintenance orders, the difficulties of enforcement and the central role played by social security in financial provision for separated and divorced spouses and their children.[13] Marsden's pioneering study of separated wives dependent on national assistance in 1965 found that only 40 per cent of the women in his sample had secured a mainten-ance order against their husbands and that only half of those with maintenance orders were paid regularly.[14] A Bedford College survey of matrimonial proceedings before magistrates courts in the mid-sixties revealed that no maintenance orders reached the statutory limit, 38 per cent of orders were in arrears for more than six weeks and fewer than one-quarter of attachment of earnings orders were fully effective.[15] The findings demonstrated that defendants in matri-monial proceedings before the magistrates courts came from the poorest stratum in society and could not maintain their families because they earned too little. The authors concluded that what was required was a recognition that the husband's obligation to maintain is in many cases a fiction.[16] The state, they argued, should assume responsibilities for payment and recovery of maintenance.

The Finer Committee on One-Parent Families in the UK concluded in 1974, on the basis of further Bedford College research and a Home Office survey which revealed that two-thirds of wives with children were awarded maintenance at a rate less than the rate of national assistance, that it was 'inevitable' that a large number of wives and mothers with court orders would have to resort to supplementary benefit (formerly national assistance and now income support).[17] Further research on maintenance in the magistrates courts in the 1980s found that over three-quarters of orders for wives with children had amounts less then supplementary benefit rates and that only 34 per cent of orders were clear of arrears.[18] A survey in 1980 of 189 divorced women who retained care and control of their children found that although 73 per cent of the women were receiving some maintenance, in only 12 per cent of cases was this their sole source of income and 25 per cent of women in receipt of maintenance were also dependent on supplementary benefit.[19] The findings, the authors concluded, highlighted the distinction 'between the middle- and upper-income groups for whom the debate about maintenance for ex-wives may still have relevance, and the remainder of the population who are likely to be caught in the poverty trap'.[20]

Carol Smart, on finding similar patterns in Sheffield magistrates courts in 1980 where only 23 per cent of wife's orders were equal to or above supplementary benefit rates, concluded that the courts were operating more or less as collecting agencies for the state.[21] It was important, she argued, to reiterate the low levels of maintenance awarded because first, they reveal the inadequacy of private and individual income maintenance and second, this empirical data 'serves to challenge the increasingly pervasive but erroneous belief that wives are parasitical upon their former husbands'.[22] Eekelaar and Maclean, in a detailed survey of a sample of the divorced population interviewed in 1981, found that in none of the childless divorces did income transfer take place at the time of interview but that income transfers took place in 36 per cent of divorces involving children.[23] Only 7 per cent of lone mothers, however, received maintenance which constituted more than half their household income and yet in over half of these cases the maintenance paid did not affect the care-giver's household income at all because she was in receipt of supplementary benefit and so the payment went either directly to the state or reduced the amount of benefit to which she was entitled.[24]

The number of lone parents dependent on income support in the UK increased from 330,000 in 1980 to 770,000 in 1989.[25] Bradshaw and Millar found that maintenance forms less than 10 per cent of lone parents' total net income, compared to 45 per cent for income support and 22 per cent for net earnings.[26] A survey of maintenance awards by the courts and the Department of Social Security local offices revealed an average weekly maintenance award of £16 per child.[27] The average weekly maintenance awarded by the courts for a spouse was £29.[28] Two out of five maintenance orders in the magistrates courts were found to be in arrears.[29]

In the United States, Lenore Weitzman's study of the financial circumstances of divorcing couples in California is perhaps the most quoted study as it reveals dramatic consequences for women and children.[30] Women and children, she found, experience a 73 per cent decline in their standard of living in the first year after divorce while men experience a 42 per cent increase.[31] Men, she found, typically do not pay alimony for the support of their former wives and pay only meagre child support. Weitzman, a Professor of Sociology at Harvard, found the research on child support in the US to produce three consistent findings: no study showed even half of fathers complying with child support orders; many fathers pay irregularly and are often in arrears; and between one-third and one-quarter of fathers never make a single payment.[32] While most American researchers agree that women are more likely to suffer a loss in economic status after marriage breakdown, there is wide disagree-ment on how big the differences are. Sorensen, also a Professor of Sociology at Harvard, believes that a reasonable guess would place the average change somewhere between a decline of 30 per cent and

10 per cent for women and a somewhat similar increase for men.[33] A survey of OECD member countries revealed that the majority of post-divorce, lone-parent households do not rely to any significant extent on private maintenance payments.[34] They formed a small part of an income package made up from state benefits and the mother's earnings. It was concluded that the part played by family law in supporting lone-parent families through private child support obligations is small and lack of compliance with support obligations, for whatever reason, is a universal problem.

This mass of empirical evidence forms the basis of the claim that divorce impoverishes women and children. These are the studies that are thought to expose the financial reality behind the legal rhetoric of divorce. This is the financial reality which we are told is avoidable by retaining the constitutional prohibition on divorce. The economic reality which is exposed by these statistics is indeed stark. If these financial consequences could be avoided by the retention of a constitutional provision then it would indeed be a valuable one. Article 41.3.2 of the Irish Constitution provides no such defence.

THE EMPIRICAL EVIDENCE IN IRELAND

The first study of the practical operation of the existing maintenance laws in Ireland reveals patterns long established in other countries: low maintenance awards coupled with high default rates.[35] A nationally representative sample of 636 maintenance orders made in the District Court under the Family Law (Maintenance of Spouses and Children) Act 1976 were examined. Although the 1976 Act is couched in gender-neutral terms, 99.5 per cent of applications were made by the wife and 86 per cent of wives in the sample had dependent children living with them at the time of application.

Sixty per cent of maintenance orders for spouses were for amounts less than the rate of supplementary welfare allowance, the lowest social welfare payment. Amounts less than the rate of deserted wife's benefit accounted for 81 per cent of orders. A large majority of wives seeking maintenance from their husbands would thus be better off in receipt of social welfare. That does not mean, however, that they can ignore the maintenance order and simply claim the welfare payment. Qualification for the relevant welfare payment will, as we shall see, depend upon continued pursuit of the husband for whatever maintenance has been awarded.

Despite the low levels of the awards of maintenance, default was high. Three-quarters of all maintenance orders were found to have arrears of six months or more and over one-quarter of the orders had never been paid. Only 13 per cent of maintenance orders were paid up to date at the time of the study. The study reveals that the enforcement procedures proved successful in only a minority of cases. While an attachment of earnings order doubled the chances of compliance, three-quarters of all maintenance awards on which an attachment of earnings order had been made were in arrears. Only when the arrest and committal to prison procedure was invoked repeatedly did it improve the rate of compliance, but even then the majority of maintenance orders remained unpaid. The inescapable conclusion is that a large majority of wives granted maintenance orders cannot be assured of an adequate or secure income and an inevitable consequence for many is long-term reliance on state support.

A simultaneous study of the deserted wive's social welfare schemes revealed that the majority of claimants of those payments were already in receipt of a social welfare payment and were attempting to qualify for another one paid at a higher rate. Only 27 per cent of claimants were assessed as having any means at the date of claim and the amount of means in most of these cases was quite low. The failure rate was 39 per cent and the majority of unsuccessful claimants were refused payments on the grounds that the husband had not deserted or that they had not made reasonable efforts to seek maintenance from their husbands, or both. Only 14 per cent of claimants had secured a maintenance order against their husbands and only 7 per cent of that number actually received the amount ordered. The deserted wive's schemes failed to address the needs of a large proportion of separated wives and their children who look to the state for a secure and regular income.

It is clear that what are described by some as the economic consequences of divorce are in fact the economic consequences of marriage breakdown. Professor William Binchy stated in 1984 that the 1976 Act

> runs completely counter to the philosophy of divorce based on breakdown of marriage. The Act seeks to protect the maintenance rights of women as effectively as possible whereas no-fault divorce seeks to release the divorced husband from his full responsibility to maintain his first wife.[36]

He argued that the introduction of divorce brought inevitable pressure for the maintenance rights of divorced women to be limited or abolished and that this development made it difficult to defend the imposition of spousal maintenance obligations during the currency of marriage. Rather than protecting us from adverse financial consequences, however, the constitutional prohibition on divorce would appear to have lulled some of us into a false sense of security whereby the belief is sustained that we do not share the problems long recognized and debated elsewhere. It is now beyond question that not only do we share these problems but that they exist to a greater degree here than in some jurisdictions with long experience of divorce.

It is important that we can now categorically refute the assertion that it is divorce which impoverishes women and children. Separated women and children already live in poverty in Ireland. It is against this background that we must examine how we determine support obligations at present and consider those proposals for reform which have emerged in the context of the revived debate.

3. The Obligation to Support One's Spouse

Article 41 of the Constitution provides that the state recognizes the family as the natural primary and fundamental unit group of society; the state guarantees to protect the family in its constitution and authority as the necessary basis of social order and as indispensable to the welfare of the nation and the state; the state recognizes that by her life within the home, woman gives to the state a support without which the common good cannot be achieved; the state pledges itself to guard with special care the institution of marriage upon which the family is based. Nowhere in the Constitution, however, do we find mention of any obligation of a spouse to support the other spouse, less still any indication of the precise nature or extent of any such obligation.

The origins of the legal obligation in Irish law of a person to maintain his or her spouse are to be found in the English common law duty of a husband to maintain his wife. The precise basis of the obligation is unclear but the biblical metaphor whereby upon marriage man and woman become 'one flesh' has been cited as the source of the doctrine of the legal unity of husband and wife which incorporates the legal existence of the wife into that of her husband.[37] Support for this contention has been found in judicial declarations that the wife in relation to her husband was 'bone of his bone, flesh of his flesh and no man did ever hate his own flesh so far as not to preserve it'.[38] While the common law thus declared the duty to exist, the enforcement thereof was deemed to be something that was within the exclusive jurisdiction of the ecclesiastical courts of the Established Church wherein all matrimonial matters were litigated after the Reformation until the nineteenth century.[39]

The ecclesiastical courts did not enjoy jurisdiction to grant a decree of divorce as commonly understood – a divorce *a vinculii* (from the bonds of marriage). From the seventeenth century onwards, however, the state provided for the dissolution of marriage by means of Private Act of Parliament.[40] A parliamentary practice developed that no divorce would be granted to a husband unless he had made adequate financial provision for his wife. Parliament ensured that the wife was not left destitute, even if she had been guilty of matrimonial misconduct, and it required the husband to make property available to secure the annual amount payable to her. While this procedure constituted a mechanism whereby the wife might secure financial support from her husband, the remedy was available only to the extremely wealthy and powerful in society. The Private Act procedure was abolished in England in 1857 but continued to apply in Ireland until suspended by the Free State Dáil in 1922[41] and rendered obsolete by the prohibition on divorce in the 1937 Constitution.

The ecclesiastical courts of the Established Church could make an award of maintenance only as an ancillary order to a decree of divorce *a mensa et toro* (divorce from bed and board), otherwise known as judicial separation. Such a decree did not dissolve the marriage – it merely relieved the spouses of the legal obligation to cohabit and it could be awarded upon proof of adultery or cruelty. Alimony could be awarded as an ancillary order to a decree of judicial separation and this was usually an annual sum calculated as a proportion of the husband's income. In 1870 the matrimonial jurisdiction of the courts of the Church of Ireland, the Established Church in Ireland, was transferred to the civil courts. The remedies available to spouses remained unchanged and the cost of instituting proceedings for a judicial separation were such that only the very wealthy could afford to pursue the remedy. A similar transfer of jurisdiction had already taken place in England in 1857 with the vital distinction that divorce was then made available there by court decree for the first time.

The Married Women (Maintenance in Case of Desertion) Act 1886 provided the first matrimonial financial remedy in Ireland which was not the exclusive preserve of the wealthiest in society This Act allowed the court to award weekly maintenance to a wife but only upon proof that her husband had deserted her and that he had refused or neglected to support his wife and children though able to do so. The remedy was originally available in the magistrates court and, after 1922, in the District Court, which as the court of lowest jurisdiction is the most accessible in terms of time and cost. The 1886 Act remained the most important legislation governing support obligations in Ireland for ninety years. The establishment of the Free State did not lead to any reappraisal of the principles to be applied to spousal support obligations and the primary concern of the first Free State government in the area of family law was to exclude the possibility of divorce.

In the 1970s a number of bodies made recommendations for reform of the outdated law of maintenance. The Commission on the Status of Women recommended in its 1972 report that the legal obligation to support the family should rest on both the husband and the wife according to their means and capacity. The Commission gave no indication as to what the nature or extent of this maintenance obligation should be other than to state that it should be for the court to decide whether reasonable arrangements had been made between the spouses as to the disposal of the family income. The Committee on Court Practice and Procedure published a report in 1974 entitled *Desertion and Maintenance* which focused on the concept of 'family default' as the basis of the support obligation. The Committee defined 'family default' as including the failure of the spouse who is responsible for the support of the family to provide a reasonable standard of living for its members having regard to the means and earnings of that spouse.

The Committee went on to express the opinion that in the long term it would be more desirable that all orders for maintenance should be met in the first instance by the local authority or the Department of Social Welfare and so relieve the spouse obtaining the order from the worries and uncertainties often associated with the implementation of such orders. In this way the state would effectively guarantee payment of whatever amount the court had ordered in each individual case, rather than making a welfare payment at a standard rate. State policy in relation to the family has been consistent in placing the primary duty to maintain within the family and ensuring that the state's role in maintaining family members is secondary and activated only upon default in relation to that primary duty. The Committee on Court Practice and Procedure seemed to be unaware of the reversal of long-standing policy implicit in its recommendations in this regard and made no attempt to rationalize them in any detail. In these circumstances, it is hardly surprising that they were not acted upon. The Minister for Justice rejected the proposal on the grounds that it would inevitably mean discrimination in the distribution of public monies between individuals based on a judgement in a private court case and that the local authorities were already in a position to assist families in need irrespective of any court order.[42]

The Minister, on introducing the Family Law (Maintenance of Spouses and Children) Bill in the Dáil, did claim, however, that the bill drew heavily upon the Committee's report and represented 'fundamental and far-reaching changes in our family law'.[43] Spousal support was placed on a gender-neutral footing and failure to provide such maintenance as is 'proper' in the circumstances became the basis of the new jurisdiction. Much emphasis was placed in the debates on the bill on the wide discretion to be given to judges in order 'to accommodate the wide range of human conflict'. This emphasis on judicial discretion led to the rejection of proposals that a proportion of a spouse's income be specified in the Act as the amount of maintenance to be ordered, for either spousal or child support. Similar proposals have since found favour, as we shall see, in the US, Australia and the UK. The new attachment of earnings procedure included in the Bill was heralded as the most effective means of enforcement. It can be invoked only upon proof of default under a maintenance order

and cannot be ordered at the same time as the making of the maintenance order, although the White Paper contains a proposal to such
effect. The problem of devising effective enforcement procedures
was recognized and somewhat pithily and pessimistically summarized
by the Minister in the following terms: 'If a husband is determined to
evade his responsibilities and disappear – no law in the world can
prevent him from so doing.'

The 1976 Act came into force on the 6 May 1976 and provided
for maintenance by way of periodical payments only. The court will
in most cases assess a weekly or a monthly amount and has no
jurisdiction to award a lump sum. In determining what constitutes
'proper' maintenance the court must have regard to 'all the circumstances of the case' and, in particular, to the following matters: the
income, earning capacity, property and other financial resources of
the parties, including statutory income or benefits with the exception
of certain social welfare payments; the financial and other responsibilities of the spouses towards each other and any children of either
or both of the spouses; and the conduct of the spouses if it is such
that the court believes it would be unjust to ignore it.[44]

This is the full extent of the statutory guidance given to the
court on whether and how much maintenance is to be awarded in
any case. The District Court is limited to awards of £200 per week
for the support of a spouse and £60 per week for the support of a
child.[45] There is no limit to the amount which the Circuit Court may
order. All hearings under the Act are held in private and, as written
decisions of the lower courts are extremely rare, there is an almost
complete lack of information on how the legislation operates in
practice. The occasions upon which the High Court and the Supreme
Court have had an opportunity to interpret the Act have been
relatively few and yet whenever the higher courts have had such an
opportunity they have consistently avoided setting down any firm
principles to be applied in the lower courts. The judges have thus
avoided setting down any specific method of calculation of 'proper'

maintenance. While 'proper' maintenance in the case of a wealthy respondent may be much more than is necessary to provide for the basic necessities of life, the courts will in most cases be concerned with meeting the needs of the parties involved.[46] The decisions of the higher courts have ensured that the lower courts enjoy the widest possible discretion in assessing how these needs are to be met.[47]

The 1976 Act did constitute fundamental reform of our maintenance law but we have seen how it has failed to ensure an adequate and a secure income for those who invoke its provisions. The starting point for any discussion on maintenance orders in this country must be that which was discovered in England over twenty years ago: that in many cases the husband's obligation to maintain is a fiction.[48] Further far-reaching reforms have since taken place in our maintenance laws with the enactment of the Judicial Separation and Family Law Reform Act 1989. The 1989 Act has been heralded as the comprehensive legislation which can now allay the fears that were raised during the 1986 divorce referendum on the questions of maintenance and property rights. It is important, then, to be clear exactly what remedies are provided by the 1989 Act and to attempt to ascertain how effective they might be. The Act was introduced as a Private Member's Bill, was accepted by the government and endured a tortuous and, at times, acrimonious passage through the Oireachtas. It represents an amalgam of the recommendations for reform of judicial separation of the Law Reform Commission[49] and the Joint Oireachtas Committee on Marriage Breakdown,[50] and draws heavily upon the English statutory provisions governing the jurisdiction of the courts to make property and maintenance orders after a divorce decree. The Law Reform Commission did not embark upon any searching enquiries into how the maintenance remedy was working under the 1976 Act but did recommend that the 1976 Act be used as the basis for the award of maintenance in the revised judicial separation law. The Law Reform Commission further recommended that the court have jurisdiction to make orders for the payment of lump sums and for the transfer of property, but only with the consent of the spouses.

The Joint Oireachtas Committee on Marriage Breakdown built its recommendations on maintenance obligations upon the fallacious premise that 'the Family Law (Maintenance of Spouses and Children) Act 1976 has operated reasonably well'.[51] The Committee did accept, however, that the law was not without faults and it went on to make 'observations' as to possible areas for change. It expressed concern at evidence of judicial inconsistency in the administration of the law in the area of maintenance and emphasized the importance of uniform judicial interpretation as to the levels of maintenance awards. The Committee neither elaborated upon how it thought judicial consistency might be attained in this area nor did it give any opinion on what proportion of a husband's income should form the basis of a maintenance award for a spouse and/or any children. A uniform approach in the adjudication of family disputes was, however, one of the main objectives of a new unified Family Court recommended in the report. The most innovative features of the proposed model included the appointment of specially selected judges solely to hear family cases, the provision of suitable training for judges and family lawyers, and the establishment of a comprehensive welfare service to be attached to the new court.[52] While the establishment of such a court would undoubtedly represent an improvement on the current decision-making structures in family disputes, its potential impact on the level and the degree of compliance with maintenance awards is impossible to predict.

The Oireachtas Committee did, however, make radical proposals for reform in order to address the problem of maintenance default. No reforms were proposed to increase the rate of compliance on the part of defaulters but the Committee recommended that the state should be empowered to make payments of maintenance to victims of default and to recoup the money owed by defaulters.[53] This was justified on the grounds of the time and expense involved for litigants in pursuing maintenance defaulters and the need to balance this 'against the constitutional responsibility placed on the state to protect marriage and the family'. No more elaborate justification was forth-coming and the proposal was made without any appreciation of the full extent of default since revealed. No mention is made of social welfare payments and how these might relate to any power on the part of the state to make maintenance payments to victims of default. The recommendation simply provides that the state be empowered to pay to the wife such amount as has been determined by the court. In this way the recommendation of the Committee on Court Practice and Procedure in 1974 has been repeated. Both recommendations suffer, however, from an apparent inadvertance on the part of the committees concerned to the fundamental reversal of state policy on the family which they would herald. In so far as they advocate placing the primary duty to maintain spouses and children after marriage breakdown upon the state, the recommendations are the most radical and possibly the most effective method of tackling the widespread poverty which has been revealed. Neither report, however, presented a comprehensive analysis of the issues involved and in some respects the recommendations appear to have been made unwittingly. It can be no surprise, then, that the proposals discussed in the two para-graphs devoted to this issue in the Oireachtas Committee's report have not been implemented.

4. THE JUDICIAL SEPARATION AND FAMILY LAW REFORM ACT 1989

The 1989 Act reformed the decree of judicial separation and extended the grounds upon which it could be granted to include grounds that do not require proof of fault on the part of either spouse. A decree may be granted upon proof of one or more of the following: adultery; behaviour such that the applicant spouse cannot be expected to live with the respondent; desertion for one year; separation of the spouses for one year, with the respondent's consent to the decree; separation of the spouses for three years; marriage breakdown to the extent that the court is satisfied that a normal marriage relationship has not existed for at least a year.

The Act came into operation on 19 October 1989 and in its first year of operation almost half of the decrees granted were successful on the grounds that a normal marriage relationship had not existed for at least a year.[54] The effect of a decree of judicial separation is simply to relieve the spouses of the legal obligation to cohabit, something of which the parties may relieve themselves by agreement. The purpose of most applications under the Act will be to invoke the greatly widened jurisdiction of the courts to make financial and property orders.[55] The court, at the time of the granting of the decree or at any time thereafter, may make a periodical payments order which is the equivalent of a maintenance order under the 1976 Act. The Act goes on to provide for the first time for lump sum orders to be made and allows for maintenance orders to be secured on any assets or property which a spouse may own. The court may make any one or more of such periodical payments orders, secured periodical payments orders and lump sum orders.

A fundamental reform of Irish matrimonial property law is effected by the introduction of a 'property adjustment order', whereby a spouse may be ordered to transfer to the other spouse or any child any property which the spouse owns. The property which may be the subject of a property adjustment order is not limited to the family home. Indeed, there is no restriction on the type of property involved and it may thus, for example, be property which was acquired prior to the marriage or property which was acquired by way of gift or inheritance. The court may also confer on one spouse either for life or for such other period as the court may specify the right to occupy the family home to the exclusion of the other spouse, and/or it may make an order for the sale of the family home subject to such conditions as the court considers proper. The court may extinguish the succession rights of either spouse in respect of the other, and such extinguishment will depend upon the provision made for the future security of the spouse in question.

The court, in deciding whether to make any of these ancillary orders and, if so, in what manner, is required to ensure that such provision is made for any spouse and for any dependent child of the family 'as is adequate and reasonable having regard to all the circumstances of the case'.[56] The Act then sets out an extensive list of matters to which the court must in particular have regard, and this list includes:

> the contributions which each of the spouses has made or is likely in the foreseeable future to make to the welfare of the family including the contribution made by each spouse to the income, earning capacity, property and financial resources of the other and any contribution by looking after the home or caring for the family;

> the effect on the earning capacity of each spouse of the marital responsibilities assumed by each during the period when they lived together and, in particular, the degree to which the future earning capacity of a spouse is impaired by reason of having relinquished or foregone the opportunity of remunerative activity in order to look after the home or care for the family.

These considerations allow the court to recognize the work of a spouse in the home and to make an award which reflects the contribution which such work constitutes towards the acquisition of not only the family home, but any property of the other spouse and, potentially more importantly, the income and earning capacity of that spouse. The Act also requires the court to examine the economic sacrifices which a spouse may have made in order to look after the home or care for the family and in this way may compensate a spouse for the losses which she has thereby incurred. The 1989 Act thus represents progressive reform in so far as it recognizes the economic impact upon, and the contribution of, a spouse who works in the home. The nature and extent of such recognition is something that is left within the discretion of the court in the context of its overall task which is no more specific than to make such provision as is adequate and reasonable in all the circumstances of the case.

The 1989 Act sets out neither specific principles underlying the obligation to maintain nor goals to be achieved by the courts in making ancillary orders. A decree of judicial separation does not dissolve the marriage and thus, because the parties retain the status of spouses, the incident of that status which requires one to support the other remains. It is perhaps understandable, then, that the wide judicial discretion bestowed by the 1976 Act is replicated in the 1989 Act. Upon the introduction of divorce, however, it shall be encumbent upon the legislature to define with much greater precision the nature of the financial duty which one person owes to another who is no longer his or her spouse. The nature of the obligation to support one's children may continue completely unaltered by the dissolution of one's marriage but the same cannot be said of the obligation to maintain someone who is now one's former spouse.

The principles governing financial provision after divorce have been the subject of prolonged debate elsewhere. When the English Divorce Reform Act 1969 came into operation the court was directed in making financial orders to place the parties in the financial position in which they would have been had their marriage not broken down.[57] This position which allowed the termination of the legal status of marriage but prevented the termination of the financial obligations came under increasing attack as being unjust and inequitable. The English Law Commission accepted the need for reform in this area and examined as possible alternative models: the relief of need; the financial rehabilitation of the parties; a mathematical approach; and the restoration of the parties to the position they would be in if the marriage had not taken place. The Law Commission eventually recommended that the duty on the court to place the parties in the financial position in which they would have been had the marriage not broken down be removed and replaced by an obligation on the court to give first consideration to the welfare of any child of the parties together with a duty to consider the 'clean break' option whereby both parties might become self-sufficient as soon as possible after the divorce.[58] These recommendations were implemented by legislation in 1984.[59]

The pursuit of the 'clean break' in the United States led to spousal support awards being made for short periods of time after which the ex-wife was expected to become financially independent. These provisions have been shown to leave women, after the expiry of the order, without either spousal support or adequate earnings and the empirical evidence of this has led to a review of the 'clean break' principle.[60] The Irish White Paper on Divorce completely fails to address this issue other than to adopt the criteria employed by the 1989 Act of 'adequate and reasonable' provision in all the circumstances of the case and incorporating these into the proposed legislation governing post-divorce support obligations. The proposal that spousal support obligations continue completely unaltered despite the termination of the legal status of marriage is indefensible. The difficult process of grappling with the principles which might most justly illuminate this area has not yet begun in this country.

In the Judicial Separation Act 1989 we have eschewed the strict 'separate property' regime whereby each spouse retained ownership of such property as was his/hers and whereby the status of spouse incorporated no right to a share in the property of the other. The courts now have the discretion to make such property awards as they see fit and they may make orders in respect of any property belonging to either spouse. It is ironic to recall the central role which the issue of property played in the 1986 referendum when the far-reaching reforms embraced in the 1989 Act were not the subject of widespread public debate. The anti-divorce lobby argued that the introduction of divorce would ultimately threaten the integrity of the family farm as the courts would inevitably be given power to distribute property as they saw fit. The image of the disintegration of holdings which have passed intact through generations proved to be quite an emotive one. The inherent inconsistency in the use of such an argument to oppose a judicial discretion to distribute family assets while at the same time predicting economic ruin for women and children after divorce did not prevent its deployment. Such arguments did not gain prominence in 1989 and the family farm may now be the subject of a property adjustment order in the same way as any other property.

The evidence which we have of the operation of the 1976 Act immediately leads us to question how effective the new maintenance and property adjustment orders will be in providing an adequate and secure income for women and children after separation. It is clear from an examination of the provisions of the Act that the effectiveness of the remedies introduced is dependent upon the ownership of property or assets on the part of one or both spouses. In the absence of any such property or assets, there is no reason to suppose that the problems of low maintenance awards and high default rates will be in any way alleviated by this enactment. The periodical payments orders, secured periodical payments orders, lump sum orders and property adjustment orders, and the matters to be taken into account by the court on application for same, mirror closely those contained in the English legislation governing post-divorce financial and property provision.[61] The availability of such remedies in England has not alleviated the plight of those women and children who find themselves in poverty after divorce. It has been found that fewer than one in five of divorced couples had savings of over £500 at the time of the divorce and that for one-third of couples the real problem was how to deal with debts, not assets.[62] It was concluded that 'rules about asset sharing on divorce, to which so much academic (and legislative) attention has been paid, though obviously necessary, will clearly have little relevance to the overall economic state of post-divorce life of most people, especially those with children'.[63] There can be no doubt but that this statement holds true for judicial separation in Ireland. Instead of learning from the experience of other countries, we appear to be falling into traps long-recognized as such elsewhere. While we must of course devise rules for the distribution of property on divorce, we seem reluctant to undertake the difficult task of actually attempting to define exactly what we mean by matrimonial property and to face up to the reality that the formulation of such rules cannot provide a comprehensive answer to the economic consequences of marriage breakdown.

The current debate in Ireland has focused upon the law governing the ownership of the family home and other matrimonial assets. The First Statement of the Second Commission on the Status of Women recommended that the family home be owned jointly by both spouses. This has been set out as a specific proposal in the White Paper on Divorce and the government has committed itself to its implementation in advance of the referendum. The Commission did go significantly further in its report where it recommended that all income during the marriage should be owned jointly by the spouses.[64] The basis of the recommendation, in the absence of a comprehensive analysis of the issue, appears to be that it would combat inequality in marriage while also being in accordance with the values underlying the prevailing notion of marriage as an economic partnership. The Commission made no detailed recommendations on how such a law might operate in practice and did not offer any definition of income.

Professor Lenore Weitzman has identified a 'discernible trend' in the United States towards recognizing what she calls 'career assets' as part of marital property, and indeed often the most valuable part.[65] She defines the term 'career assets' as including:

> a large array of specific assets such as pensions and retirement benefits, a professional education and licence, enhanced earning capacity, medical and hospital insurance, goodwill value of a business, entitlement to company goods and services, and government benefits such as social security.

Weitzman argues that if they have been acquired during the course of a marriage they should be included in the pool of property to be divided upon divorce. The Irish White Paper on divorce recognizes that loss of entitlement to a prospective occupational pension may cause hardship for women after divorce.[66] It offers no solution on the point, however, other than to state that the court ought to have an overall discretion to refuse a divorce decree on the grounds of hardship. Some comfort seems to have been taken in the White Paper from the fact that no means has yet been discovered in the UK of equitably dividing pensions. It fails, however, to discuss initiatives in other jurisdictions which have attempted both to recognize pension rights as marital property and to devise methods of dividing entitlement thereto.[67] The problem of pension splitting is discussed briefly and in isolation in the White Paper – no reference is made to similar benefits and entitlements which may be termed 'career assets'. The problem of devising a just method of dividing pension entitlements can only begin to be solved when it is placed in the context of the general debate on the definition of marital property, which debate has yet to commence in this country.

The 1989 Act does provide for a more equitable distribution of property after separation and for more effective enforcement of maintenance obligations – but only where sufficient property or assets, as understood in the traditional sense, are held by spouses in the first place. Where insufficient property or assets are available for distribution or for securing maintenance, the Act merely invokes the pre-existing enforcement mechanisms available under the 1976

Act which have been shown to be ineffective, for whatever reason, in the majority of cases in which they have been invoked. The Judicial Separation Act does not provide a comprehensive legislative response to the problem of poverty on marriage breakdown. Such a comprehensive response is impossible in legislation which focuses solely on the distribution of property and finance as between the parties.

Jurisdiction to grant decrees of judicial separation under the 1989 Act is bestowed upon the High Court and the Circuit Court, which is to be known as the 'Circuit Family Court' when exercising its jurisdiction in family law matters. A proposed amendment to the Bill on its passage through the Dáil to confer jurisdiction on the District Court was defeated.[68] It was argued in favour of the amendment that in order for the remedy and the new ancillary orders to be accessible to all, jurisdiction should be granted to the court where proceedings were the least expensive and most expeditiously completed. The rejection of the amendment was justified on the grounds that the judges of the Circuit Court are more qualified than those of the District Court to determine proceedings with consequences as far-reaching as those of judicial separation; that a unified family court should ultimately be established and that provision in the 1989 Act for a multiplicity of courts with jurisdiction in this area would not assist that goal; and that the problem of unequal access to justice should be addressed by an expanded legal aid scheme.

Neither the range of orders under the 1976 Act nor the matters to be taken into consideration on the making of such orders were affected by the Judicial Separation Act.[69] While the Circuit Court retains its jurisdiction under the 1976 Act, its jurisdiction over financial and property matters has been greatly increased under the Judicial Separation Act. In view of the fact that Circuit Court proceedings are much more expensive than those in the District Court and that the civil legal aid scheme is grossly inadequate, the choice of maintenance remedy will be determined by ability to pay. By retaining the maintenance remedy under the 1976 Act almost totally unamended while introducing a more extensive one under the Judicial Separation Act, we have embedded more deeply in our legal system the discriminatory features of family law which have persisted for over a century. Despite the enactment of the Judicial Separation Act, little has changed for the majority of separating couples, who do not have significant assets. There is no reason to hope that the cycle of low maintenance awards and high rates of default will cease. In the absence of a greatly expanded legal aid scheme, the District Court will continue to cater for the majority of wives and children who seek financial support from their husbands and fathers.[70]

The problems identified in the empirical research on maintenance in the District Court have resulted in the 1992 White Paper proposals that the 1976 Act be amended to allow the courts to make secured maintenance orders and lump sum orders in addition to the periodical maintenance orders. Such reforms would represent a welcome extension to the jurisdiction of the District Court and allow for greater flexibility in the orders that it may make. The government further proposes to allow the courts to make attachment of earnings orders at the time of the making of the maintenance order. This proposal is a direct response to the evidence that attachment of earnings orders double the chances of compliance with maintenance orders. It represents one of the few substantive reforms proposed in the White Paper which specifically address the central issues of low maintenance and high default. The White Paper otherwise simply proposes the adoption of the Judicial Separation Act as the basis of the new divorce law and those ancillary orders which are now available after judicial separation would thus be available after a divorce decree.

5. SOCIAL WELFARE PROVISION

The difficulty of establishing an adequate and secure income from within the resources of the parties means that there can be little doubt but that social welfare payments will constitute the main source of income of a great number of divorced women and children. The White Paper remains silent, however, on the role of social welfare payments in the determination of the standard of living of parties to divorce and on the relationship between any such payments and maintenance. The persistent reiteration and proven emotive potency of the assertion that divorce causes poverty for women and children must be met by a detailed analysis of the current relevant social welfare payments and the formulation of comprehensive proposals on how our welfare code will be reformed to accommodate divorce. The White Paper summarizes some of the relevant provisions and states that these arrangements 'would, of course, fall to be reviewed' in the light of divorce.[71] We are given no indication whatsoever as to what the nature of any such review might be and the issue is abandoned to the vagaries of the course of the divorce debate as it was, to such costly effect, in 1986.

The hardship suffered by deserted wives and children was deemed to be sufficiently serious and widespread a problem as to warrant the introduction of a new social assistance scheme in 1970, the deserted wife's allowance. This allowance was an attempt to deal with the income needs 'in the long term' of the deserted wife and her children and claimants were to be treated as if they were widows claiming non-contributory pensions and thus desertion had to be 'firmly established and more or less permanent' as widowhood is in the case of widow's pension.[72] A social insurance payment, deserted wife's benefit, was introduced in 1973 in response to criticism that the equation of the deserted wife to the widow was incomplete in the absence of a payment equivalent to the widow's (contributory) pension. No more elaborate justification than this was given for the extension of social insurance to the area of marriage breakdown. A social assistance payment was introduced for unmarried mothers in 1973 but no social insurance payment followed for this category of claimant. A claimant of a deserted wife's payment who is under forty years of age must have at least one dependent child living with her. A woman will be regarded as deserted by her husband for the purposes of these payments if he has 'of his own volition left her' and if he is paying her no maintenance or an amount less than the rate of the welfare payment. In order to qualify for payment she must make and continue to make 'appropriate efforts' to obtain maintenance from her husband.

The deserted wife's allowance is, as with all social assistance payments, means tested and any income above £6 is assessed as means. In order to qualify for the deserted wife's benefit, on the other hand, the claimant must satisfy a social insurance contribution requirement. This contribution requirement may be met on either the husband's or the wife's record but they may not be added together. The deserted wife's benefit has always been the preferable payment because, as with all social insurance payments, it was not means tested and it thus allowed recipients to work without a reduction in the rate of payment. In 1992, however, in one of the most controversial welfare reforms in a year of cuts in public expenditure, a means test was imposed on a social insurance payment for the first time when it was provided that a claimant of deserted wife's benefit earning more than £14,000 a year will not qualify for the benefit and a claimant earning between £10,000 and £14,000 a year will qualify at a reduced rate.[73] This reform represents an abandonment of what had hitherto been a fundamental principle, and indeed the distinguishing feature, of social insurance payments whereby no means test is imposed upon claimants. It is of further interest to us that the deserted wife's benefit was chosen as the first social insurance income maintenance scheme to be restricted in this way.

The Report of the Commission on Social Welfare in 1986 constituted the first comprehensive review of the social welfare system in Ireland.[74] The Commission based its recommendations for a reformed welfare system on five principles: adequacy; redistribution; comprehensiveness; consistency; and simplicity. It is essential, the Commission stated, that identical needs and circumstances are so far as possible dealt with identically and that the welfare system should not alter people's basic choices regarding general lifestyle or choice of living arrangements.[75] Having proposed the retention of the existing social insurance/assistance system, the Commission recommended a comprehensive social assistance scheme covering all existing assistance categories and any other persons who had an income need. The same level of payment should apply to all recipients of social assistance, it was proposed, and the application of the means test should be uniform. The Commission then went on to examine specific categories of welfare recipients and chose one-parent families as one such category. A continued rise in the number of deserted wives and unmarried mothers was projected and it was recognized that family life and household structures in Ireland are undergoing change. The Commission noted that lone-parent families headed by women rely to a significant extent on welfare payments rather than earnings and that at that time many lone parents did not qualify for payment under any of the 'lone-parent' schemes.[76] The factors which contributed to female lone parents' reliance on welfare rather than earnings were identified as the concentration of women in low-paid, low-status employment, employment-related costs, the need to arrange and pay for child-care and the role which women have traditionally played in caring for children.

In addition to the recommended changes in the basic payment structures, the Commission addressed a number of specific issues in provision for lone parents. The Commission stated its support for the principle that the primary obligation to maintain one another rests with the marriage partners and that the state's role is to intervene only where maintenance cannot be secured or is inadequate. It did recognize, however, that the reality for many women receiving maintenance under a court order or separation agreement is that payment 'is often irregular and uncertain'.[77] The Commission nevertheless questioned whether or not a social insurance payment for deserted wives was justified and concluded that while the case for income support may be clear cut, it was not clear that this support should be provided by an insurance scheme. While it was not convinced that desertion could be regarded as an insurable contingency, it did recognize that any attempt to make alternative income maintenance provision must take account of the acquired rights and entitlements of those currently in receipt of deserted wife's benefit. It was for this reason, it would appear, that the Commission fell short of recommending the abolition of the benefit. The Commission's comments have served to undermine the continued existence of the benefit and it is unfortunate that a fuller examination of the relative merits of social insurance and social assistance for lone parents was not undertaken.

The Commission recognized the difficulties which many women face in enforcing maintenance orders and proposed that the state should have power to award a deserted wife's benefit or allowance and itself pursue outstanding maintenance claims, but only where payment is irregular or uncertain. It did not discuss the possibility of removing in its entirety the burden from the wife of pursuing her husband. The empirical evidence now to hand lends support to the argument that a claimant should be relieved of an onerous and often fruitless task which may be carried out solely in order to fulfil a qualifying condition for a social welfare payment. The Commission, when recommending that the Department pursue a defaulting husband, made no mention of what was to become of any maintenance thereby obtained. The silence on this point is to be regretted because, in the absence of any recommendation, legislation has been enacted which alters radically the treatment of maintenance payments in welfare provision for lone parents.

The central issue in this area, the Commission determined, is whether a dependent spouse is being adequately supported finan-cially, and the form or cause of the marriage breakdown should not be a relevant consideration. It was for this reason that it was recommended that the desertion condition be dropped from the benefit and allowance. This condition has posed great difficulties for many claimants and its removal is central to any attempt to treat all lone parents alike. The Commission did not follow through upon the logic of its recommendation to this effect and it was not stated whether it should be replaced with a requirement of proof of separation or whether the payments should now be extended to all lone parents. It was made clear that the Commission believed that its recommendations for the re-structuring of social assistance in terms of the income needs of claimants rather than on the categorical basis which exists at present should entitle all lone parent families who experience an income need, regardless of the cause of lone parenthood or the sex of the parent, to a social assistance payment. It would be necessary, it was stated, to establish whether or not a woman was being adequately supported by her husband, but the 'rigid criteria' surrounding proof of desertion would be unnecessary.

It is clear that the Commission envisaged social assistance as the optimum method of addressing the income needs of lone parents. The deserted wife's benefit was tolerated because of the difficulties associated with its removal, yet at the same time it was recommended that it be expanded to encompass at least all separated wives. The Commission was not unaware of the anomalies which would persist under its reformed schemes and recognized that there may be a case for a more unified approach to social welfare provision for all lone-parent families. The divorce referendum was pending at the time of publication and the Commission stated that if divorce were introduced, a more thorough review of income support provision for lone parents would have to be undertaken.

The recommendation of the Commission that social assistance be payable to lone parents irrespective of the cause of the lone parenthood or the sex of the parent was implemented in 1990 with the introduction of the lone parent's allowance. The lone parent's allowance (LPA) is designed to provide a single payment for all lone parents and thus eradicate the complex categorization of parents within social assistance while at the same time lifting some lone parents from dependence upon supplementary welfare allowance, the lowest welfare payment. Some assistance payments have thus been subsumed within the new allowance and others have been replaced in part to the extent that they provide for persons bringing up children alone. The unmarried mother's allowance has been subsumed in its entirety within the new payment while the deserted wife's allowance and the widow's (non-contributory) pension have been abolished as separate payments to the extent that they apply to claimants with dependent children. They continue to apply, as before, to deserted wives who do not have dependent children. Deserted wife's benefit remains completely unaffected by the new allowance and there is no extension of social insurance for lone parents in these reforms.

A lone parent is defined for the purposes of the new allowance as someone who is a widow, a widower, a separated person, an unmarried person or a prisoner's spouse where the period of committal is not less than six months. There must be at least one child normally residing with that person where the child is under eighteen years of age or is between eighteen and twenty-one years of age and is in full-time education.[78] The regulations define a separated spouse as one who is not being maintained by the other spouse or is being maintained, but at a rate less than the relevant rate of lone parent's allowance.[79] A separated spouse must, in order to qualify, make and continue to make 'appropriate efforts' to obtain maintenance from the other spouse for him or herself and for their children. The allowance is, of course, means tested and is payable at the full rate where the weekly means do not exceed £6. The Department allows a further £312 per year for each child which is not counted as means if it derives from earnings and allowances are also available for child-minding and travel expenses in connection with work.

The lone parent's allowance represents a progressive reform of social assistance in so far as it provides a unified payment for persons bringing up children alone, irrespective of the sex of the parent or the cause of the lone parenthood. Its most immediate practical impact has been to lift two categories of lone parent off supplementary welfare allowance: women who were disqualified from deserted wife's payments on the ground that they had failed to prove desertion and men who were bringing up children alone. The concept of desertion retains its importance, despite the proposals of the Commission, for claimants of deserted wife's benefit and the 'rump' deserted wife's allowance. The possibility thus persists of two wives over forty years of age, without dependent children, ending up at opposite ends of the social welfare payments scale. One such wife, having proved desertion and an adequate insurance record, could qualify for deserted wife's benefit at the maximum rate, retaining any earnings under £10,000. Another such wife, without means or employment, and who cannot prove desertion or an adequate insurance record, could end up dependent upon supplementary welfare allowance.

The Social Welfare Act 1989 introduced new provisions governing liability to maintain one's family incorporating a new definition of a liable relative. For the purposes of the lone parent's allowance, the deserted wives schemes and supplementary welfare allowance, a person is liable to maintain his or her spouse and is liable to maintain any child under eighteen years or between eighteen years and twenty-one years if in full-time education.[80] A 'liable relative' of anyone in receipt of one of these payments is liable to contribute to the Department of Social Welfare such amount as the Department 'may determine to be appropriate towards such benefit or allowance'. There are no statutory provisions or regulations governing how the Department shall arrive at a decision on the appropriate amount which the liable relative shall pay, nor on what factors are to be taken into consideration.[81] When a determination is made, it is not appealable by notice to the Chief Appeals Officer in the normal way because it is not a decision of a Deciding Officer. The normal social welfare appeals process has thus been bypassed without any justification in relation to decisions which will inevitably be subject to challenge by dissatisfied liable relatives. Unsurprisingly, in the absence of statutory guidelines, the manner in which the Department assessed the contribution caused concern almost immediately to representatives of separated spouses.[82]

If the liable relative fails or neglects to pay the contribution, the Department may apply to the District Court for an order directing him to do so and the court may fix the amount of the contribution to be made.[83] There are no statutory guidelines governing how the court is to arrive at such a determination and extensive judicial discretion is again granted in this legislation as it is under the 1976 Act. It is important to note that while the Department may now institute proceedings against a liable relative, it is not obliged to do so. A spouse who claims one of these social welfare payments is still required to make efforts herself to obtain maintenance in order to qualify and where a maintenance order has been granted to her, she must transfer to the Department payments made under that order.[84] If a person fails to transfer payments in this way then the benefit or allowance may be reduced by the amount which was liable to be transferred. It is impossible to justify the imposition of the emotional and financial strain of court proceedings on the claimant rather than the Department. The legislation fails to allow a wife to assign her maintenance rights, and the power of enforcement thereof, to the Department and thus free herself from the process of pursual, while at the same time it deprives her of any financial benefit she might derive from a maintenance order. A new unit has been established within the Department of Social Welfare for the purpose of pursuing liable relatives and it remains to be seen how effective the extended powers of the Department and the courts will prove to be in the attempt to enforce the private obligation in order to reduce welfare expenditure.

6. INTERNATIONAL TRENDS

The cost of welfare payments for the inexorably rising number of lone parent families has led to the issue of child support coming into sharp focus in the family policy of many western countries. Recent legislative initiatives have set the goal of increasing the level of financial support provided by the non-custodial parent, whether married to the custodial parent or not. The most noticeable trend has been away from judicial discretion in the assessment of maintenance obligations and towards either statutory guidelines on the amounts to be awarded or the formulation of statutory formulae to be applied by government agencies, thus bypassing the judicial process altogether. Whatever the level of support set, the important issues remain of enforcement and of the relationship in a broader sense between state and individual responsibility for the economic support of lone parent families. Maclean points out that the state may adopt a residual policy and intervene with varying levels of social action – the most minimal state tactic being to leave an aggrieved recipient to use the legal process against any debtor.[85] The next step is to invest public funds in pursuing private resources, and tentative steps towards such an approach have been introduced here in cases where social welfare payments are being made. A further major step is for the state to guarantee payment to the receiving household and then pursue the debtor.

The report of the Finer Committee published in the UK in 1974 was the first comprehensive analysis of the economic position of lone parents and it continues to repay reading after almost twenty years.[86] The Committee proposed a new welfare payment which would address the special needs of one-parent families and, in particular, three factors which stood out when considering the financial position of lone parents. These were the lack of any worthwhile financial gain by combining part-time work with social security; the low level of income among working one-parent families compared with two-parent families; and the inadequacy and uncertainty of maintenance payments as a source of income.[87] In considering what form of state help was needed for one-parent families, the Committee set out six principles which should underpin such provision.[88] The help needed should be:

1. a replacement, so far as the recipient is concerned, for maintenance payments, so that lone mothers should be freed from the worry and distress which the inadequacy and uncertainties of these payments now produce;

2. large enough to offer the lone parent a genuine choice about whether or not to work;

3. designed to provide effective help for those with part-time or low full-time earnings;

4. of universal application; that is, it should be available to all kinds of one-parent families, without discrimination, since all are at a disadvantage;

5. simple to claim, and avoiding face-to-face interviews, searching enquiries and constant reporting of changes;

6. equitable, in the sense that it should not tip the scales too far in favour of one-parent families as compared with low-income two-parent families.

On the basis of these principles the Finer Committee recommended the introduction of a new welfare payment called guaranteed maintenance allowance (GMA). The payment was to be means tested because the Committee felt that for an insurance payment to be available to as many lone parents as possible, the contribution conditions would have to be so liberal that the insurance principle would be 'stretched so thin as to become somewhat artificial'.[89] Entitlement to the payment would depend only on establishing status as a one-parent family. The GMA was to be, as Eekelaar described it, 'a child's benefit',[90] and a mother's right to GMA would arise by virtue only of her having care of a child, not by virtue of her status as a wife or ex-wife.[91] Eekelaar felt that it may be part of a general movement in family law away from considering the spouses' rights as between themselves as central to one treating the welfare of the children as central.[92]

The GMA was designed to be a substitute for maintenance payments, which would be assessed and collected by the authority administering the allowance; they would be offset against the allowance paid and any excess would be paid to the mother.[93] In this way it was felt the need for lone mothers to go to court to sue for maintenance would be largely eliminated. The Committee proposed that the social security authorities should assume the whole responsibility of recovery from the liable relative 'by making an administrative order against him by reference to uniform and disclosed principles, and by applying to the courts for enforcement of the order as appropriate'.[94] The benefit was to become payable without regard to whether or not the mother seeks or obtains a maintenance order on her own account. In this way, her support 'becomes entirely a matter of public law'.[95] In order to give lone parents a genuine choice about whether or not to work it was to be paid at a higher rate than supplementary benefit and was to be payable whether or not the recipient was in full-time work. There was to be an initial earnings disregard, after which a portion of the excess was to be deducted from the adult part of the allowance and it would taper off until earnings reached about the level of average male earnings.[96] The child portion of GMA would remain payable, however, irrespective of earnings and this was seen as a contribution by the state to all one-parent families to help with the extra cost of caring for a child where one of the parents is not available.[97] The recommendations of the Finer Committee have, however, never been implemented in the UK and the reason most often given for this failure is one of cost.

The fact that women bear the risk of the adverse consequences of breakdowns in the child-rearing system in disproportion to men reflects society's social organization of labour.[98] Since the deprivations are, at root, socially caused, society (not the individual women) must bear the responsibility and it can thus be forcefully argued that the burden of this insurance should lie primarily on the state. The welfare provision now made in Ireland for lone parents and deserted wives is worth examining in the light of the six principles enunciated by the Finer Committee, despite the fact that the recommendations were never implemented. In relation to the first principle, both the deserted wife's payments and the lone parent's allowance operate as a replacement for maintenance. If maintenance is paid at a rate greater than the rate of DWA/LPA, the claimant will not qualify for a payment. A wife is not, however, freed from the burden of pursuing her husband for maintenance, as such efforts remain a qualifying condition to payment. The state may however, relieve her of this task and the repeal of the regulations requiring appropriate efforts to be made by her is required.

The second and third principles state that the payment should be large enough to offer the lone parent a genuine choice about whether or not to work and that it should be designed to provide effective help for those with part-time or low full-time earnings. In Ireland there is a high rate of unemployment among lone mothers, yet a large proportion of them would like to work. The deserted wife's benefit is paid at a rate which is amongst the highest of all welfare payments, the recipient need show no inability to work, and all earnings under £10,000 are disregarded. In this respect the deserted wife's benefit gives the wife a very real choice about work and a secure base from which to enter the workforce. It is not, however, of universal application amongst wives, much less lone parents, and the 'desertion' condition has been retained despite recommendations for its abolition. It also falls foul of the fifth principle which requires a payment to be simple to claim and to avoid searching enquiries. The 'desertion' condition necessitates the most searching of enquiries and proves very difficult to satisfy. The sixth principle requires that the payment be equitable, in that it should not tip the scales too far in favour of one-parent families as compared with low-income two-parent families. The total disregard of all earnings can place a recipient of DWB, who is in full-time employment, at a considerable advantage over a low-income two-parent family.

The lone parent's allowance meets the criteria set out in the last three principles in that it is of universal application, is relatively easy to claim and does not advantage one-parent families over two-parent families inequitably. It does not, however, give the recipient any real choice about work. The earnings disregard of £6 per week and a further £6 per week for each child, before deductions are made in proportion to earnings, are insufficient to provide effective help for women with part-time or low full-time earnings and operate as a disincentive to work for a recipient. The allowances for 'reasonable' childcare and travel costs incurred as a result of employment are important additions. But it is the level of the disregards which will most influence the employment patterns of the recipients.

The argument that the state should make provision for women who have suffered financially as a result of child-rearing but who no longer have dependent children, has long been accepted here in the case of deserted wives. Both deserted wife's benefit and allowance are payable to women over forty years of age who have no dependent children. While this provision in deserted wife's benefit is open to criticism in that there is an assumption of financial dependency on the part of the wife, the principle of recognizing the financial cost to the wife of the assumption of her role in the marriage is a sound one. Again the condition of desertion applies and must be abolished. There is no condition that the wife must have had children, let alone the care of them, or that she worked in the home at the expense of employment opportunities. It is important to remember, in the context of the divorce debate, that the deserted wives' payments would not, without amendment, be payable to a divorced woman as she is no longer a 'wife'. If our welfare code were to remain unchanged upon the introduction of divorce, the lone parents allowance would become the only social welfare payment of relevance to a divorced woman. The erosion of the financial protection available to women after marriage breakdown which this would represent can only be avoided by further reform of our welfare code. The approach taken in New Zealand of providing benefit to a person who had the care of a child or children for a given number of years can produce a benefit payable irrespective of the marital status of the claimant.[99] Reforms of this nature would address the needs of lone parents in a way in which recent legislative initiatives have failed.[100] The international trend, however, is to focus, not on the needs of lone parents, but on ways of reducing welfare expenditure in respect of them.

The concern of governments to curtail growing public expenditure on one-parent families has led to profound changes in child-support law. The child-support systems established in the US, Australia and now Great Britain, share as their primary goal a reduction in the reliance of lone parents on social security payments. The method by which such a reduction is to be achieved is the vigorous enforcement of the maintenance obligations of fathers. The trend is now towards a replacement of judicial discretion in the determination of maintenance awards by standard formulae and the enforcement of such awards by state agencies, using attachment of earnings as the favoured method.[101] The legislation in America has focused on: obtaining awards in nearly all child-support cases; determining the award in the overwhelming majority of cases by a numeric standard; regularly updating the award to reflect changes in the ability to pay of the absent parent and the needs of the child; requiring that child-support payments be made to a public agency; requiring that child-support payments be withheld from wages and other sources of income in every case. On these issues it has been concluded that 'the country is moving away from judicial discretion toward the standardization associated with taxation and social insurance'.[102] Such a movement has now taken place in Australia and Great Britain.

Over twenty-five years after the publication of the Finer Report, the British government has initiated fundamental reform of the law in relation to child support. The government's proposals were set out in a White Paper, *Children Come First*, published in October 1990,[103] and within ten months the Child Support Act 1991 became law. The White Paper set out the case for fundamental change of the system of child support by listing a number of problems which arise in the present system.[104] They lie in the fact that lone-parent families are forming an increasing proportion of all families (14 per cent in 1987 compared to 8 per cent in 1981); that a growing proportion of them is receiving income support (66 per cent now compared to 40 per cent in 1979); and that the proportion of lone parents going out to work is falling.[105] While Eekelaar accepts that the evidence in the White Paper on maintenance awards shows 'a wide "scatter" of the value of child support awards', he points out that the evidence does not relate their value to any spousal maintenance order, nor is there any indication whether the debtors were supporting other children.[106] For these reasons, he states that it is difficult to share the government's certainty that financial orders, taken together, are 'too low' and while it may well be that the new scheme will bring in more money from absent parents, that must remain largely speculation.

The main features of the proposed package are:

> a formula for the assessment of how much maintenance should be paid which will apply to all families where maintenance is an issue and therefore eliminate any scope for inconsistency,

> a child support agency which will have responsibility for tracing absent parents and for the assessment, collection and enforcement of maintenance payments. The agency will be there to provide these services for all families to use.

Under the new scheme, which came into operation in April 1993, the courts will no longer have responsibility for assessing and reviewing child maintenance claims in most cases.[107] The courts will continue to have jurisdiction over spousal maintenance and related matters which arise on divorce or separation including residence of and custody and access to children and property settlements. The child support agency will identify and trace liable persons and assess the amount of maintenance by applying the statutory formulae.[108] It will collect and monitor payments, and have responsibility for the enforcement of 'child support maintenance'.[109] Payments may be made direct to the caring parent or through the agency[110] and the assessment of the amount of child support maintenance will be subject to periodical review.[111] The agency will have power to prescribe the method of payment of maintenance and may order it to be paid by way of deduction from earnings.[112] Any person seeking maintenance for the benefit of a child may use the services of the agency.[113] Where a caring parent is in receipt of social security benefits, however, she shall be required to authorize the agency to take action under the Act.[114] The British government expects that when the agency is fully operational up to 200,000 more lone parents will receive maintenance regularly and about 50,000 caring parents will no longer be dependent on income support.[115]

The British government concluded that maintenance should not be in any way disregarded for caring parents who are receiving income support.[116] Income support is thus left unreformed under the new scheme. There is no extension of social security cover for lone parents but rather the hope that the reformed system will lift 50,000 lone parents off income support. Even if this were to occur 700,000 lone parents will remain reliant upon income support and, unless in receipt of one of the three benefits for working persons, will enjoy no advantage from increased maintenance payments from the liable person. The impetus for pursuing fathers and ex-husbands stems from a growing number of one-parent families and the ensuing cost to the state, 'combined with a swell of moralizing . . . which states that "while marriages break down, parenthood goes on forever"'.[117] The Legal Action Group said that the White Paper represented 'an unacceptable conflation of benefits policy and child maintenance reform' and that the attempt to devise a combined approach was praiseworthy but inadequately thought out.[118] The proposals, it said, did not properly consider the role of capital payments or arrangements in relation to the family home and their implementation would save the Department of Social Security money but would not necessarily benefit children.

While the English Law Society welcomed the formula for calculating maintenance payments, it wished to see the system operated by the courts rather than the child support agency, or alternatively the agency could deal with child support if there were no other financial matters to be settled.[119] The director of the National Council for One-Parent Families was of the view, however, that the two main strands of the reform, the formula and the agency, give more hope to lone parents that maintenance will be paid at reasonable levels than the 'discredited' court system.[120] Eekelaar argues that the courts should retain a residual role for mothers not on benefit who wish to go there and that the courts should be permitted to depart from the formula level where this would be in the child's interests and otherwise just and reasonable.[121] The Child Support Act 1991 contains no such provision. The concern of the British government is quite obviously to reduce growing public expenditure rather than to improve the position of lone parents. Whether the scheme will actually have the effect of improving the position of significant numbers of one-parent families remains to be seen.

The Australian child support scheme was introduced as a result of research showing the poverty of mothers rearing children alone and the 'phenomenal blowout in social security payments to supporting parents in the last decade'.[122] The office of Child Support Registrar was established in 1988[123] as part of the tax office and maintenance orders and court-registered agreements are recorded as 'registrable maintenance liabilities'. Once registered the liability becomes a debt to the government and can only be enforced by the registrar, the usual method of collection being deduction from wages. The use of the tax office facilitates the tracing of liable relatives through income tax records and it has details of employers as a result of its administration of PAYE. The child support obligation is determined by a formula which is to be applied administratively and is intended to apply in the majority of cases. After a self-support component (set at the single rate of social security pension, or higher if he has dependent children living with him) is deducted from his taxable income, a percentage deduction is applied at rate of 18 per cent for one child, 27 per cent for two children, 32 per cent for three, 34 per cent for four and 36 per cent for five children.

A Child Support Evaluation Advisory Group was established to monitor the new scheme and it reported in 1990 that the average levels of child maintenance had increased substantially and that the proportion of sole-parent welfare recipients receiving maintenance had increased to 36.5 per cent, compared to 25.6 per cent before the scheme began.[124] It is estimated that the formula produced awards that were on average about one-third higher in real terms than the pre-scheme arrangements and that compliance on the part of absent parents assessed under the agency rules was at an estimated rate of 70 per cent.[125] Millar and Whiteford describe the short-term gains of the Australian scheme as real but modest.[126] Almost half of those registered under the scheme are not receiving payments and non-payment for many reflects an inability to pay because of unemployment. They believe that the scheme has probably been most successful at increasing payments from those who would be most likely to pay anyway.

Stephen Parker states that to regard the scheme as a solution to child poverty would be 'wildly optimistic' but it should result in some increase in the standard of living for many children.[127] The scheme seems to benefit, he states, those custodians who are already in work more than those reliant on social security. Whilst custodians wholly reliant on social security lose some or all of their payment when child support is paid, those who are working lose no child support until their earnings exceed average weekly earnings.[128] This, Parker feels, is probably the result of the government's desire to improve work incentives for sole parents. The emphasis on relieving the taxpayer of the burden of supporting lone parents resulted in the withdrawal of support for the scheme from welfare groups and women's organizations.[129] Regina Graycar points out that despite the Australian government's commitment to ending child poverty by 1990, the scheme will only assist those families where there is a liable parent with a capacity to pay.[130] Children without fathers, or whose fathers have no money, will receive no additional income support and no corresponding measures to assist those unable to avail themselves of the scheme have been announced.[131] The Australian Council of Social Service and the Women's Electoral Lobby withdrew their support for the scheme when it became clear that there would be no 'advance maintenance guarantee', payable in respect of every child in a one-parent family and irrespective of whether it is possible to secure maintenance from the father.[132]

The British White Paper singles out the state of Wisconsin as being foremost amongst American states in the development a child support enforcement programme.[133] The programme in Wisconsin is distinct from those in other states because: it uses immediate witholding of wages from absent parents; it uses a maintenance formula based on a percentage of income, rather than judicial discretion; and it has been looking at the possibility of introducing a child assurance system, offering a guaranteed minimum amount of child support for all lone parents.[134] It is reported that the routine witholding of wages from absent parents has increased the number of child support payments by 4 to 6 percentage points and the amount of payments by between 11 and 30 per cent.[135]

A federal child-support enforcement programme was established in the US in 1975.[136] A federal Office of Child Support Enforcement (OCSE) was established and each state was obliged to set up a corresponding agency to help enforce child-support in all cases where the lone parent was in receipt of public assistance, called Aid to Families with Dependent Children (AFDC). Each state was required to maintain a parent locator service that tied in with the federal service, which has access to social security, internal revenue and all other federal information resources except census records. AFDC applicants must assign their rights to uncollected child support to the state and must agree to co-operate in identifying and locating absent parents, in obtaining maintenance orders and in securing payments and unjustified failure to co-operate results in withdrawal of AFDC benefits. The states were required to adopt expedited procedures for obtaining support orders either through the judicial system or an administrative agency. The primary goal of the new enforcement system was to reduce the federal cost of the AFDC programme. It was then recognized that this goal could be more easily attained if potential recipients of AFDC were kept off welfare by extending the support enforcement programme to them.[137] Since 1980 support enforcement has been available to everyone and this has made a 'significant difference' in middle-class family support and more than half of the collections made go to families who are not on welfare.[138] Between 1976 and 1985 collections for AFDC families increased by 282 per cent.[139]

Reforms to the programme were made in 1984 in order to further strengthen enforcement powers. State laws must now provide for attachment of earnings if there are arrears of one month's payments; provision must be made for the imposition of liens against the property of defaulting parents; and arrears of support must be deducted from federal and state tax returns. The 1984 amendments also required states to establish discretionary guidelines for child-support awards in an attempt to achieve greater consistency in the levels of award made. An amendment was made to the means test for AFDC whereby the first $50 per month of child support is now disregarded and paid directly to the recipient. The 1988 amendments to the programme provide that by 1994 all new or varied support orders are to be deducted automatically from the absent parent's wages. Support guidelines must be used as the presumptive level of child-support awards and all support orders are to be reviewed every three years. A number of states, most notably Wisconsin, went beyond federal law and introduced schemes similar to those now in operation in the UK and Australia.

7. CONCLUSION

The international focus in devising legislative responses to the problem of poverty after marriage breakdown has been on the public enforcement of the private duty to maintain. The arguments that have won the day on the replacement of judicial discretion with numerical standards are that the public has a legitimate interest in the standard of living of a child, particularly when low support may result in increased public expenditure; that the traditional system results in inequity when awards are left in the hands of individual judges; and that the traditional system exacerbates tensions by placing the determination in an adversarial context. Garfinkel and Wong argue that making the child support award a rebuttable presumption would be a compromise which would eventually promote much greater uniformity while still preserving a fair degree of judicial discretion. The lack of information on the husband's income in court files in Ireland has meant that we cannot conclude from the District Court data that maintenance awards are too low. On this point we can hopefully learn from the experience in Britain whether the application of a statutory formula produces greater equity in determining maintenance obligations or whether it produces hardship for the non-custodial parent. In the meantime, we have a system which allows almost total judicial discretion in the determination of what constitutes 'proper' maintenance. Neither the legislature nor the courts in Ireland have been prepared to set any guidelines for the assessment of either spousal or child support.

Few maintenance awards in Ireland are varied and their real value decreases with inflation. The argument for moving away from the judicial process for the variation of awards because of the time and expense involved is unanswerable. The indexing of awards using the consumer price index would retain the value of the original order while the judicial process could be retained as an option for either party to seek variation on the grounds of change in incomes.

It is argued that the trend towards making the collection of maintenance more akin to the collection of taxes is a bureaucratic encroachment on private life.[110] The counter-argument is that default on maintenance obligations is widespread and that the involvement of a state agency increases rates of compliance. It is further argued that automatic attachment of earnings is the most effective method of enforcement and justified on the grounds that the obligation to support one's children is a paramount responsibility. There is no doubt now that default on maintenance orders constitutes a crisis in the operation of family law in Ireland and that women and children are suffering as a result of non-payment of awards. Public enforcement of maintenance obligations in this country plays a secondary role and is only available to recipients of social welfare payments. A state agency which would undertake the enforcement of all maintenance awards made or approved by the courts could only increase the rate of compliance and reduce the stress and anxiety suffered by those who seek their dues alone.

While the arguments for increasing the levels of child support and the strengthening of the enforcement procedures have been enthusiastically embraced by the governments of the countries we have examined, it has been left to voices on the sidelines to point out the limitations of private support. Garfinkel and Wong estimate that even if the maximum could be achieved from private support in the US, it would leave unsolved three-quarters of the poverty and welfare dependence of one-parent families. They argue for an assured maintenance benefit which, when combined with earnings, would lift many lone-parent households out of poverty and remove them from welfare because it is designed to supplement rather than replace earnings.[141] They cite in support of their argument the case of Sweden, where almost all custodial mothers are in the workforce. Sweden's advance maintenance system provides a guaranteed minimum payment, set at 40 per cent of the official basic need of a child, in respect of all children with an absent parent. They make no mention, however, of the very low rate of unemployment enjoyed by Sweden or the extensive state-supported child-care services which combine to make employment for custodial mothers a much more realistic option than it is in Ireland.

Just as Australia and Britain have adopted the approach initiated in the US since the mid-seventies, questions are now being raised by those who initially enthusiastically supported it. Professor Harry Krause, one of the architects of the federal programme, has concluded that in the US '[o]ur justified insistence on the enforcement of the father's un-met legal obligation has unjustifiably eclipsed the need to understand that adequate support of children is a public necessity'.[142] Child-support collection, he stated, 'has turned into an income transfer program from poor fathers to lawyers and welfare bureaucrats – something I hoped we would avoid'[143] and the current emphasis on enforcing the father's obligation has clouded judgement on how much the father can realistically be expected to provide. Now that the 'national non-enforcement scandal' has been alleviated, he argues that it is time to consider whether a 'social relationship factor' would be appropriate in the definition of appropriate child-support.[144] Graycar addressed this issue in her criticism of the Australian scheme which, she said, presumed that all children are born into a uniformly constituted family which survives, in some form or another, even after the relationship between the parties has broken down.[145] There was no place in this structure, she argued, for any recognition that not all children are born in the context of a marriage-like relationship between a man and a woman. Krause is concerned that there is a movement toward a fractured society in which the needs of children are met neither by parents nor the government and he calls for a 'much more effective public contribution' of services and finance to assure basic necessities and a fair start in life for every child.[146]

Western countries, as Eekelaar and Maclean commented, 'have been tenacious in retaining the ideology that a child should look first to its parents for the retention of its living standards, even after the collapse of the family unit'.[147] It was not until social security bills grew dramatically, however, that many countries began to examine how that ideology translated into practice. The most common response thus far has been the limited one of attempting to ensure that the father reimburses the state to the greatest extent possible for public expenditure on the mother and children. It is clear that reform of matrimonial property laws and stronger enforcement of the duty to maintain will not, alone, alleviate the poverty of the growing numbers of lone-parent families. State policy must focus clearly on the central issue of the needs of children and their carers and move in from the penumbra of simply 'making fathers pay'.

In Ireland, successive governments have been reluctant to admit that we share, in common with the rest of the western world, the phenomenon of rapidly changing family structures and the associated problem of widespread poverty among lone parents. The evidence of how our law operates in practice demonstrates in stark terms how income-generating rights on marriage breakdown fail to provide an adequate and secure standard of living for spouses and their children. Recent reforms of family and social welfare law have perpetuated the piecemeal and incoherent approach which has characterized the legal regulation of the financial consequences of separation in Ireland. The fallacious and mischievous notion that the retention of the constitutional ban on divorce obviates the necessity for a reassessment of our family policy must be rejected. The introduction of divorce in Ireland does provide, however, an obvious opportunity for such a reassessment. A uniform and comprehensive policy on income maintenance for lone parents and separated and divorced persons, drawing on the experience of those jurisdictions in which support laws have been radically overhauled, yet rooted firmly in the needs of the individuals and their children, must now begin to be formulated and is urgently required.

Notes

1. Article 41.3.2 provides that 'No law shall be enacted providing for the grant of a dissolution of marriage.'
2. The proposed provision was as follows: 'Where, and only where, such court established under this Constitution as may be prescribed by law is satisfied that:
   i   a marriage has failed,
   ii the failure has continued for a period of, or periods amounting to, at least five years,
   iii that there is no reasonable possibility of reconciliation between the parties to the marriage, and
   iv any other condition prescribed by law has been complied with, the court may in accordance with law grant a dissolution of the marriage provided that the court is satisfied that adequate and proper provision having regard to the circumstances will be made for any dependent spouse and for any child who is dependent on either spouse.'
3. The turn-out from an electorate of 2,440,907 was 60.4 per cent.
4. See summary of arguments of both sides of divorce debate in *Report of the Joint Committee on Marriage Breakdown* (1985) (Pl. 3074, Stationery Office), paras. 7.8.11 and 7.8.12; for detailed arguments of both sides see William Duncan, *The Case for Divorce in the Irish Republic* (I.C.C.L. Report No. 5, revised edition 1982) and William Binchy, *Is Divorce the Answer?* (Irish Academic Press, Dublin, 1984). See also 14, 15, 16 and 21 May 1986) 366 *Dáil Debates*, Cols. 790–856; 919–990; 1022–1067; 1077–1113; 1218–1354; 1356–1466; 1609–1667; 1694–1750; 1752–1802; 1881–1942; 1977–2018.
5. A question on whether or not one was separated was not included in the national census until 1986.
6. *Census 86: Summary Population Report* (Stationery Office, 1987).
7. *Labour Force Survey 1991* (Stationery Office, 1992).
8. *Census 91: Summary Population Report – 1st Series* (Pl. 9743, Stationery Office).

9. *Statistical Information on Social Welfare Services* (Pl. 8806, Stationery Office).

10. *Health Statistics 1991* (Stationery Office).

11. Millar, Leeper and Davies, *Lone Parents – Poverty and Public Policy in Ireland* (Combat Poverty Agency, 1992).

12. Davis, Macleod and Murch, *Divorce: Who Supports The Family?* (1983) 13 Fam Law 217, p. 217.

13. See Denis Marsden, *Mothers Alone – Poverty and the Fatherless Family* (Revised Edition, Pelican Books, 1973); O.R. McGregor, L. Blom-Cooper and C. Gibson, *Separated Spouses* (London, Duckworth, 1970); *Report of the Committee on One-Parent Families* (Finer) (Cmd 5629, Her Majesty's Stationery Office, 1974); Colin Gibson, *Maintenance in the Magistrates' Courts in the 1980s* (1982) 12 Fam Law 138; Davis, Macleod and Murch *Divorce: Who Supports the Family?* (1983) 13 Fam Law 217; Carol Smart, *The Ties That Bind* (London, Routledge & Kegan Paul, 1984); John Eekelaar and Mavis Maclean, *Maintenance After Divorce* (Clarendon Press, Oxford, 1986); Edwards, Gould and Halpern *The Continuing Saga of Maintaining the Family After Divorce* [1990] Fam Law 31; UK White Paper, *Children Come First* (Cm. 1264, HMSO, 1990) vol. 2.

14. Marsden, *Mothers Alone*, op. cit., p. 197.

15. McGregor, Blom-Cooper and Gibson, *Separated Spouses*, op. cit., pp. 81, 93 and 106.

16. ibid., p. 215.

17. Finer, op. cit., para. 4.83.

18. Colin Gibson, *Maintenance in the Magistrates Courts in the 1980s* op. cit.

19. Davis, MacLeod and Murch, *Divorce: Who Supports the Family?* (1983) 13 Fam Law 217.

20. ibid., p. 224.

21. Carol Smart, *The Ties That Bind*, op. cit., p. 199.

22. ibid., p. 194. See also Edwards, Gould and Halpern, *The Continuing Saga of Maintenance After Divorce*, op. cit.

23. Eekelaar and Maclean, op. cit., p. 91.

24. ibid., p. 94.

25. U.K. White Paper, *Children Come First*, vol. 2, para. 1.4.1.

26. Bradshaw J. and Millar J., *Lone Parents in the U.K.* (HMSO, 1991).

27. ibid., vol. 2, para. 4.1.1.

28. ibid., vol. 2, para. 4.1.1.

29. ibid., vol. 2, para. 5.1.3.

30. Lenore Weitzman, *The Divorce Revolution – The Unexpected Social and Economic Consequences for Women and Children in America* (The Free Press, New York, 1985).

31. ibid., p. 337.

32. ibid., p.284.

33. Annemette Sorensen, 'Estimating the Economic Consequences of Separation and Divorce: A Cautionary Tale from the United States', in Weitzman and Maclean (eds.), *Economic Consequences of Divorce* (Oxford University Press, 1992).

34. Mavis Maclean, 'Lone-Parent Families: Family Law and Income Transfers', in *Lone-Parent Families – The Economic Challenge* (OECD, 1990).

35. Peter Ward, *Financial Consequences of Marital Breakdown* (Combat Poverty Agency, 1990).

36. William Binchy, *Is Divorce The Answer?* (Irish Academic Press, 1984), p. 38.

37. Glanville Williams, *The Legal Unity of Husband and Wife* (1947) 10 MLR 16. See also McGregor, Blom-Cooper and Gibson, op. cit. and Finer and McGregor, *The History of the Duty to Maintain*, Finer Report, op. cit., vol. 2, appendix 5.

38. *Manby* v *Scott* (1663) 83 E.R. 995.

39. See William Duncan *Desertion and Cruelty in Irish Matrimonial Law* (1972) 7 I.J. 213.

40. See Finer and McGregor, op. cit.; McGregor, Blom-Cooper and Gibson, op. cit., chp. 1; Duncan, op. cit.

41. Standing Orders were amended to prevent a private Act of divorce. See J.H. Whyte, *Church and State in Modern Ireland 1923–1979* (Gill and Macmillan, 2nd edn. 1980).

42. (22 July 1975) 284 *Dail Debates*, Col. 71.

43. ibid., Col. 55.

44. Section 5(4) of the 1976 Act as amended.

45. A 'dependent child' is defined for the purposes of the 1976 Act as any child under the age of 16 years, or between 16 and 21 if in full-time education, or any child irrespective of age if that child is suffering from mental or physical disability to such extent that it is not reasonably possible for him to maintain himself. The Status of Children Act 1987 amended the 1976 Act to provide for the maintenance of children born outside marriage on a similar basis to that for children born inside marriage.

46. The courts could not grant a maintenance order in favour of a spouse who had deserted the other until the Judicial Separation and Family Law Reform Act 1989 amended the 1976 Act to allow a court to do so if it was of the opinion that it would be unjust not to make an order. The 1989 act also repealed those provisions of the 1976 Act which rendered adultery, in certain circumstances, a discretionary bar to maintenance. It replaced them with the provision requiring the court to consider conduct only if it would be unjust to ignore it. See Duncan and Scully, *Marriage Breakdown in Ireland – Law and Practice* (Butterworths, 1990), paras. 8.035–8.050.

47. See Duncan and Scully, op. cit., chp. 8. For a comparative analysis of the 1976 Act, see Paul O'Connor, *Key Issues in Irish Family Law* (Round Hall Press, 1988), Chp. 3. The Guardianship of Infants Act 1964 also grants jurisdiction to the courts to order the mother or father of a child under eighteen years of age to pay towards the maintenance of that child such weekly or other periodical sum as, having regard to the means of the mother or father, the court considers reasonable. Despite this procedure, however, the 1976 Act has provided the most commonly employed procedure whereby a wife might secure financial support for her children.

48. McGregor, Blom-Cooper and Gibson, op. cit., p. 215.

49. *Report on Divorce a Mensa et Toro and Related Matters* (LRC Report No. 8, 1983).

50. *Report of the Joint Committee on Marriage Breakdown* (pl. 3074) (Stationery Office, 1985).

51. ibid., para. 7.4.12.

52. ibid., paras. 9.5–9.7.

53. ibid., para. 7.4.13.

54. Irish White Paper, *Marital Breakdown – A Review and Proposed Changes* (Pl. 9104) (Stationery Office, 1992), Appendix 3.3.

55. For a detailed treatment of the Act see Duncan and Scully, *Marriage Breakdown in Ireland – Law and Practice* (Butterworths, 1990), chp. 13.

56. Section 20(1), The Judicial Separation and Family Law Reform Act 1989.

57. See Cretney and Masson, *Principles of Family Law* (Sweet and Maxwell, 5th edn. 1990) chp. 19.

58. The Law Commission Report *The Financial Consequences of Divorce* (Law Com No. 112, 1982) followed its Discussion Paper (Law Com No. 103, 1980).

59. Matrimonial and Family Proceedings Act 1984.

60. Weitzman L. and Maclean M., *'Economic Consequences of Divorce' – The International Experience* (Oxford, 1992).

61. Matrimonial Causes Act 1973. See Cretney and Masson, op. cit., chp. 19.

62. Eekelaar and Maclean, op. cit., p. 86.

63. ibid.

64. *Second Commission on the Status of Women* (Pl. 9557), Stationery Office, 1993), para. 2.3.1.

65. Lemore Weitzman, 'Marital Property: Its Transformation and Division in the United States', in Weitzman and Maclean, *Economic Consequences of Divorce – The International Experience*, op. cit.

66. Irish White Paper, op. cit., at p. 106.

67. See, for example, Weitzman, 'Marital Property: Its Transformation and Division in the United States', op. cit., and Voegeli and Willenbacher 'Property and Pension Splitting in the Federal Republic of Germany', also in Weitzman and Maclean, op. cit.

68. See (29 June 1988) *Official Report of the Special Committee on the Judicial Separation and Family Law Reform Bill 1987*, Cols. 293–320 and (23 Feb. 1989) *Dáil Debates*, Cols. 1411–1450.

69. Apart from the issues of desertion, adultery and conduct which we have examined.

70. There were 555 applications for judicial separation in the year 1989/90 compared with 2,273 applications for maintenance under

the 1976 Act in the District Court (Appendix 3.2, *Maritial Breakdown – A Review and Proposed Changes*, op. cit.)

71. Irish White Paper, op. cit., p. 75. For an account of the current relevant social welfare payments, see Gerry White and Mel Cousins *A Guide to Welfare Payments for Families* (FLAC, 1992).

72. (14 July 1970) 248 *Dáil Debates*, cols. 999–1000.

73. Section 100 Social Welfare (Consolidation) Act 1981 as amended by s.25 Social Welfare Act 1992; S.I. No. 237 of 1992.

74. *Report of the Commission on Social Welfare* (pl. 3851) (Stationery Office, 1986).

75. ibid., section 6.5.4.

76. ibid., section 18.2–3.

77. ibid., section 18.4.2.

78. Section 198A Social Welfare (Consolidation) Act 1981 as inserted by s.12 Social Welfare Act 1990 and s.2(1) of the 1981 Act as amended by s.7 Social Welfare Act 1989.

79. Social Welfare (Lone Parent's Allowance and other Analogous Payments) Regulations 1990, S.I. No. 272 of 1990.

80. Section 315 Social Welfare (Consolidation) Act 1981 as inserted by s.12 Social Welfare Act 1989.

81. See Mel Cousins, *Liability to Maintain* (1992) 86 ILSI Gazette 387.

82. See *The Irish Times*, 17 April 1991.

83. Section 316 of the 1981 Act as inserted by s.12 Social Welfare Act 1989.

84. Section 317 of the 1981 Act as inserted by s.12 Social Welfare Act 1989.

85. Maclean, M. 'Lone Parent Families: Family Law and Income Transfers', in *Lone Parent Families – The Economic Challenge* (OECD, 1990).

86. *Report of the Committee on One-Parent Families* (Cmnd 5629) (HMSO, 1974).

87. Finer, op. cit., para. 5.49.

88. ibid., para. 5.56.

89. ibid., para. 5.90 and 5.141.

90. J.M. Eekelaar, *Public Law and Private Rights: The Finer Proposals* [1976] Pub. Law 64, p. 69.

91. Finer, op. cit., para. 5.119.

92. J.M. Eekelaar, op. cit., p. 70.

93. Finer, op. cit., para. 5.104.

94. ibid., para. 5.185.

95. J.M. Eekelaar, op. cit., p. 70.

96. Finer, op. cit., para. 5.131–5.133.

97. ibid., para. 5.129.

98. ibid., p. 143.

99. See Eekelaar and Maclean, *Maintenance After Divorce*, op. cit., p. 112.

100. See generally on this point Millar, Leeper and Davis, *Lone Parents – Poverty and Public Policy in Ireland* (Combat Poverty Agency, 1992).

101. Garfinkel and Wong, 'Child Support and Public Policy', in *Lone Parent Families – The Economic Challenge* op. cit.

102. Garfinkel and Wong, op. cit., p. 106.

103. *Children Come First*, (HMSO, 1990) (Cm 1264, 2 vols.)

104. ibid., vol. 1, para. 1.5.

105. ibid., vol. 2, chp. 1.

106. J.M. Eekelaar, *A Child Support Scheme for the UK – An Analysis of the White Paper* [1991] Fam. Law 15.

107. Section 8 Child Support Act 1991.

108. ibid., Section 11 The Powers described as those of the 'child support agency' are conferred by the Act on the Secretary of State for Social Security. The term 'child support agency' is employed in the text in the sense in which it was employed in the White Paper and references to it are to be taken as references to the Secretary of State.

109. ibid., sections 29–41.

110. ibid., section 29(3).

111. ibid., section 16.

112. ibid., section 31.

113. ibid., section 4(1).

114. ibid., section 6(1).

115. ibid., para. 5.35.

116. ibid., para. 6.6.

117. Hayes M. *Making and Enforcing Child Maintenance Obligations – Will The Proposed Scheme do More Harm than Good?* [1991] Fam. Law 105.

118. Reported at [1991] Fam Law 45.

119. See (1991) 21 Fam Law 122.

120. ibid.

121. J.M. Eekelaar, op. cit., p. 16.

122. Mr. Justice Kay, *The Child Support Scheme* (1990) 60 Law Institute Journal 604, at p. 604.

123. The Child Support (Registration and Collection) Act 1988.

124. Millar J. and Whiteford P., *Child Support in Lone-Parent Families: Policies in Australia and the UK* [1993] Policy and Politics. See also *Australian Assessment* [1991] Fam Law 85.

125. *Children Come First*, op. cit., vol. 2, para. 7.5. See Millar and Whiteford, op. cit. for an extremely helpful comparison of the British and Australian schemes.

126. Millar and Whiteford, op. cit.

127. Stephen Parker, *The Australian Child Support Scheme* [1990] Fam. Law 210.

128. See Regina Graycar, *Family Law and Social Security in Australia: The Child Support Connection* (1989) 3 Austl. J. Fam. L. 70, p. 81.

129. See Regina Graycar, op. cit., pp. 82–85.

130. ibid., p. 82.

131. ibid.

132. ibid., p. 84.

133. *Children Come First*, op. cit., vol. 2, para. 7.3.

134. See a summary of the Wisconsin child support programme in Garfinkel and Irwin, *Maintenance Through the Tax System: The Proposed Wisconsin Child Support Assurance Program* (1986–87) 1 Aust. J. Fam. L. 152 and Aaron Bransky, 'An Unfortunate Change of Circumstances: Wisconsin Prohibits Retroactive Revision of Child Support Orders' [1988] *Wisconsin Law Review* 1123.

135. *Children Come First*, op. cit., vol. 2, para. 7.3.

136. For a summary of the child support programme and recent reforms see Harry Krause, *Child Support Reassessed: Limits of Private Responsibility and the Public Interest* (1990) 24 Fam L.Q. 1, pp. 6–14 and Garfinkel and Wong, 'Child Support and Public Policy', op. cit., chp. 6.

137. Krause, op. cit., p. 6.

138. ibid., p. 7.

139. Garfinkel and Wong, op. cit., p. 105.

140. Garfinkel and Wong, op. cit., p. 119.
141. Garfinkel and Wong, op. cit., p. 120.
142. Krause, op. cit. p. 17.
143. ibid., pp. 14–15. On this point it is worth noting that it is estimated that 2,200 new staff will be required to run the child support agency in the U.K. ([1991] Fam Law 122).
144. ibid., p. 23.
145. Regina Graycar, op. cit., p. 86.
146. Krause, op. cit. p. 33.
147. Eekelaar and Maclean *Maintenance After Divorce* op. cit., p. 109.